My Radical Encounters with Angels

Angels in the Flesh, Angels of Protection and More

Matthew Robert Payne

My Radical Encounters with Angels
Copyright © 2015 by Matthew Robert Payne. All rights reserved.

More information about Matthew can be found at
http://www.matthewrobertpayneministries.net

Matthew also can be found on Facebook in a group that he runs called "Open Heavens and Intimacy with Jesus." that can be found here
https://www.facebook.com/groups/OpenHeavensGroup/

Matthew has written several other books before this one and they can be found on his Amazon author page here:

http://www.amazon.com/Matthew-Robert-Payne/e/B008N9R896/ref=ntt_athr_dp_pel_1

Editor: Melanie Cardano from www.upwork.com

The opinions expressed by the author are not necessarily those of Revival Waves of Glory Books & Publishing.

Revival Waves of Glory Books & Publishing
PO Box 596
Litchfield, IL 62056
United States of America
www.revivalwavesofgloryministries.com

Revival Waves of Glory Books & Publishing is committed to excellence in the publishing industry.

Published in the United States of America

Paperback: 978-1-68411-236-4

Table of Contents

Dedications

The Hungry Ones

I am a hungry one. I am a person who is fascinated with spiritual things and spiritual encounters. I am constantly hungry for more of God. This book is dedicated to people who are just like me. All of those who love Jesus so much that it sometimes hurts. I long to be in the arms of Jesus and be part of the New Earth. Life can be painful until that time, but until then, I have to move and live in the river of the Holy Spirit.

If you hunger after angel stories like me, I have written this book for your enjoyment. It is my prayer that this encourages you.

Michael Van Vlymen

I also dedicate this book to an author who is one of the hungry ones. In this book, I have mentioned Michael and his books, which I suggest you read. Here, we meet a couple of angels called Michael, so I thought it fitting that the book is also dedicated to one.

Michael has a passionate faith and is a prayer warrior, and I am glad that he is one of my friends. It is my prayer that more people learn of him and his written works from this book, and they go on to be blessed by his wisdom, as I was.

God bless you, Michael, and may His angels always be at your back!

Acknowledgments

The Angels in My Life

I want to personally thank all the angels that have played a part in my life so far. I am not aware of any authors who have said thanks to their angels, but I thought this was the best place in the book to thank you, guys. I am sure that my life has been saved more times than I know. I'm certain that many angels have been involved in my personal life and ministry, so I hope Jesus can pass on my heartfelt thanks to you, my winged guardians.

Jesus

You have been a very good friend to me. Even whilst I lived a prodigal life for so many years, You were traveling by my side. Your angels guided me as I entered the brothel in Kings Cross and kept me safe for a year as I ministered your love to the prostitutes there.

I love You, as You have compassion for me and You gently lead me to lay down beside still waters. You have brought a lot of healing to my life and You continue to support me. You have taught me to minister out of rest and You continue to teach me through the Holy Spirit.

You are the best friend a person could have.

Holy Spirit and Father

I want to thank You for Your roles in my life. You are both special to me and have done great things for me. Thank you, Father, for loving me and leading me to You. Thank you, Holy Spirit for bringing order to my days and teaching me things. Thank You for inspiring me to write this book and sharing with me what stories to tell.

June Payne

Thank you for all your love and encouragement through my life. Thank you for being the best mother that a single guy like me could have. You have heard all these stories and now, other people are about to read them!

Melanie Cardano

Thank you for your belief in me and your tireless work in editing my words on a page. Thank you for being a vital part of my team in this book project. Melanie is a freelance editor and can be hired on www.upwork.com.

Bill Vincent

I want to thank Bill as he prepares my manuscripts and publishes my books for me. Bill is with *Revival Waves of Glory Books and Publishing* which can be found on Google.

Kudzai

I want to thank this lady for supporting my ministry. It is through her monthly support that I was able to get this book published.

Foreword 1

I love stories and testimonies about angels and interactions with angels. They can encourage our faith like nothing else can. God has set His angels in our lives to encourage us and help us and protect us and the awareness of that brings a measure of peace and confidence that can get us through the toughest times.

Testimonies of encounters with angels can give us a platform from which to experience these things for ourselves. The power of the testimony can literally break open these types of encounters in the lives of those who read them and desire them also. That is why Matthew Robert Payne's book "My Radical Encounters with Angels" is so important. Matthew experiences a relationship with angels that is both supernatural and normal. Supernatural in the fact that the power and presence the angels carry can be overwhelming but normal in the fact that Matthew's relationship with the angels in his life is one that is manifest in everyday living. And that's the way it should be.

I first began to listen to Matthew's testimonies of his interactions with angels well over a year ago. I was both encouraged and amazed as I heard the most amazing things that happened in Matthew's life. Matthew's honesty and transparency concerning his interactions with the angels gives powerful credibility to the testimonies he shares. He is not trying to paint himself in the most favorable way in these interactions but rather is just presenting these stories the way they occurred, therefore making them all the more accessible for the rest of us. Matthew also has gained much wisdom from these encounters which he openly shares, not only to encourage but to tell of the things that he has been taught.

I would encourage you to read about these encounters and envision what it would be like if they had happened to you. Use the testimony to prompt you to ask God for the same. And then expect it!

Michael Van Vlymen
Author – How to See in the Spirit
Angelic Visitations and Supernatural Encounters

Foreword 2

From the moment I made acquaintance with Matthew - I knew he was a special brother – that was in August 2012 or there about on Facebook- when I was invited to join a group – "Open Heavens and Intimacy with Jesus". Since then, interacting with him and other friends seeking to live under an Open Heaven and have greater intimacy with Jesus - God showed Me this radical man who was having encounters that we could expect in a glory realm on Earth in a future envisioned Kingdom setting. But the truth is that we can have it now! Men have sought and have had such experiences since Jesus said long ago - "My sheep hear My voice and follow Me "

You won't go wrong entertaining the possibility that perhaps we have been held back by those who wish to be Lords over us who prevent us from and being "Christ" in the Earth. Go ahead and read this short book – You might just find yourself raised from your slumber and you will be transformed into a glorious life and abundant living.

The Kingdom has come near to you today. As you read these accounts seek, ask and knock and it will be opened unto you. This book is not just one man's account of his interactions with angels, but it is an invitation for us all to seek God for them. With my own encounters following my brokenness God is showing me that for all who will only believe, that truly all things are possible. Every true preacher, prophet, apostle, and child of God will tell you that you need only to believe. Come just as you are and see that God is good to those who love Him. Mathew's book will help you to see that for sure.

Let Matthew's book open vistas of possibilities to you so that will roll all over the gates of hell which hold you back from receiving the Kingdom in all its glory.

Sheldon Bennett

Introduction

There are many times that angels are mentioned in the Bible. Many people in the Old and New Testaments encountered angels. Having angels interact with you should not be something weird or strange. It should be your birthright as a child of God.

The cover on this book depicts a female angel. Though only male angels are mentioned in the Bible, I have heard many testimonies of people encountering female angels. There are not a lot of angelic pictures out there and this is the picture my cover designer came up with.

As a Christian, you may feel that you *"need"* a scripture verse or two, along with every encounter, to prove that the encounters are Biblical and can be trusted. To some, it may be very disappointing and disconcerting to find that there are no Bible verses in this book. I did not feel the need to convince you through scripture that my encounters were real and that they can be trusted.

We all have a Holy Spirit that is part of our lives and He is well able to give you peace and confirm what happened to me really happened as I said. While quoting scriptures may put some people at ease, it is not going to make the stories more believable.

To the world, I am just a little guy who preaches prophetically and who likes to write books. This is my shortest book, by far, and yet I hope it is power packed enough for you.

This book has a number of my encounters. Some may be hard for you to believe and wrap your head around. And yet, as Jesus Christ is my witness, I swear they all happened to me.

This book was inspired by two books that I read by Michael Van Vlymen. Those two books are called *Angelic Visitations and Supernatural Encounters: A Diary of Living in the Supernatural of God* and *Angels and Demons: Encounters in the Unseen Realm.*

I want to make it clear that while I see and interact with angels more often than most people, I do not worship or promote them in any way in my life or ministry. After reading this book, some people won't be able to help themselves and say that I do. But their comments are not going to stop me for releasing this book.

This is not a book of doctrine; it is not a teaching book. It is simply a book of some of my encounters, in which I share to encourage people in their faith. I would love to hear from people who have also encountered angels in their journey.

Chapter 1

First Angels I Encountered

In the normal Christian life, you should live where not only there are angels in your life, but you should be able to experience angels at work in your life. It can be a very good feeling and is helpful, and very encouraging. In this short book, I am going to put together a number of stories from my life and hope that you can get some insights into the working of angels.

Story 1 Can't Go to Sleep

The first time I met an angel, I was fourteen years of age. I was not in a good place emotionally and spiritually. My youth group leader had discerned that I have some need for healing ministry to be done, what some people call today prayer ministry. And so she'd arranged for me to come in the next day and receive some healing in the morning. I was trying to sleep the night before, but for some unknown reason, I couldn't.

I went and woke my mother up, which I used to do when I was sick. I told my mother that I couldn't sleep, so she got a sleeping tablet from the medicine cabinet. She gave me one and told me to go back to bed. Obediently, I went back to bed. I laid there for an hour. Sleep was still elusive. I woke my mother up again. As a child, I didn't think about waking my mother for the second time. And I did. She gave me one more sleeping tablet and told me that I'm not to wake her up again. To be sure, she'd given me an adult dose. I went back and laid down. About an hour into it, I knew that I needed help because the sleeping tablets weren't working.

I had a relationship with Jesus at that time and I could speak to Jesus in two way conversation, which a lot of Christians can't. I asked Jesus, "What's my angel's name?"

Jesus said, "Your guardian angel's name is Michael."

So I put my hand up in the air and I said out loud by faith "Michael, hold my hand."

I realize that I had a lot of faith as a child. As an adult, not as much. As soon as I put my hand up and said, "Hold my hand", something like electricity went through my hand, and right down to my arm. I have heard people talk about the anointing coming through them like electricity. The electricity that came through my arm was the last thing I remembered. It shocked me to sleep.

The next morning, the car wouldn't start. We needed my father's help to get it to work. On the way down to the healing ministry, my mother had a nosebleed. She'd never had one before, so she knew that the attack was demonic. Because of this, she made me get out of the car and told me to cross once I reach the traffic lights. She said, "Make sure the 'Walk' sign is on and do not take any risks crossing the road without lights." I headed my way and had some healing ministry.

In this first experience, I had some of the first spiritual warfare in my life. It can be a little bit of a worry when you lay down for hours and you can't go to sleep. Satan didn't want me to go and get healing and even made sure that sleeping tablets didn't work. I don't think he counted on me calling for my angel's name and holding his hand. Many people are surprised that I know my guardian angel's name. It's really as simple as asking your angel for their name. Some people may go their whole lives and not have an angel story like this one I just covered. I want to stress right here that angels should not be a mystery to us, but they have been sent to help us.

At one stage in my Christian walk, I did not have my spiritual eyes open and could not see visions of angels. A person needs to have their spiritual eyes opened to see angels and other things in the spiritual realms. To help you open your spiritual eyes, I can suggest two books for you: *Seeing in the Spirit Made Simple* by Praying Medic, and *How to See in the Spirit: A Practical Guide on Engaging the Spirit Realm* by Michael Van Vlymen.

Story 2 Homeless Alcoholic Begs

Because I could not see through the Spirit, my next encounters with angels happened while they're in human form. It was during the time I was living in Brisbane, 600 miles north of Sydney, where I'm living now. It came one afternoon towards the end of the working day. I was walking through the city, when I met what looked like a homeless alcoholic. This figure approached and asked me if I had any change.

I had a five dollar note in my pocket and I didn't have the love in me to actually say, "Wait a second while I get some change for you." I would need to go to a shop and change the money. I needed three dollars for some milk and bread that I was going to buy at the shop near my house, so I couldn't hand over the five dollars to the man. If I cared for the man, I could have taken him to a shop with me and got two dollars change for him.

But instead of doing that, I lied to the man who'd asked me if I had spare change. As soon as he passed by me and walked on, a verse came to my mind that said, *what you do to the least of my brethren, you do onto me.*

When confronted with that verse, I turned around as quickly as anything and ran after him. He went behind a telephone box, which was a see through one, but I didn't really notice him behind it. I ran to where the telephone box was and looked for a hundred feet and he was gone. He disappeared into thin air and I was dumbfounded. I was cut to the heart and really upset that I failed Jesus, and began to walk towards home.

Jesus said to me, "You judged that man; you thought that because he was an alcoholic, he doesn't need a drink and your money. You could've changed your money, but you decided not to, because he wasn't worth it to you. You need to stop judging people. You need to learn not to judge people."

Today, if you read any book under my name, you'll find that I'm a real big advocate of giving money and support to homeless people. I have a real lifestyle of telling others that they need to do as I did. That's where it all started. My compassion came from that encounter with an angel disguised as a homeless drunk and Jesus advising me afterwards.

As I walked home, I got to a crossroad, when a man approached me and asked where a certain street was. It was about two suburbs away from the city we were in. I was a taxi driver, so I knew the street in that suburb and I described how many traffic lights he needed to reach, to get to the street he was looking for.

I said, "Go five sets of lights up that road, take a left. Then go two sets of lights, take a left and the street is the second street on your right." The businessman took ten dollars out of his wallet and put it in my top pocket. I said, "I can't take this."

He said, "I have an important appointment in that place and it's worth money to me to know where it was."

I crossed the street and started crying because now, I had fifteen dollars. It didn't occur to me yet that the first man, the alcoholic homeless man, was an angel that had disappeared into thin air. And I didn't realize that the second man was an angel, too.

I've been asked for directions hundreds of times, because my skin carries the glory of the Lord and people who need help always seem to approach me. I've never had anyone in my life besides that person give me money for directions. I believe the encounter was a lesson. Some people interact with angels and these angels teach them lessons. That was a lesson that I never forgot. That was a lesson that has truly affected my life.

The first angel caused me to learn a lesson. I learned not to judge people by the way they look, or come across. Today, when I carry cash, I always give to the poor without asking questions. One thing you need to remember about angels is that when you meet with one in human form, they don't normally tell you that they are an angel. It is for you to pick up in your spirit-man that you had an encounter.

The second angel, the businessman, was also needed. It was with that encounter that my money went from five dollars to fifteen dollars. That extra money made me cry in repentance. I knew that if I had given the first five dollars away, the extra ten dollars would more than covered what I gave away. At the time, I was not aware that both men were angels. After some time, I came to understand that they were.

These two encounters taught me not to judge people on appearances. I will never forget those encounters. Jesus really took my attention and I will never forget His words on that day. One way to judge if an encounter was real and from God is to test the fruit that came from it. Because I became a person who loves the poor and homeless, and gives to them without reservation, it's clear that these encounters bore good fruit.

Story 3 Businessman Gives Counsel

I will tell the story of the fourth angel in this chapter. I drove my taxi to Queensland University and waited for a passenger on the taxi rank. A businessman crossed the road, put his briefcase in the back of my taxi and jumped in the front. While driving out of the University, I asked him how his day was and he said he had a good one. Then he said, "We're not going to talk about me, but during this ride, we're going to talk about you."

He started asking me questions about my life. He told me to tell him the truth and he had a real caring attitude about him. He was the sort of person that is like a pastor, who really loves you. There was empathy flowing off him. I felt really relaxed talking to him and soon, I was crying and telling him that I was in a custody battle with my wife, fighting for the right to see my child. He told me that Jesus said not to take your brother to court and I shouldn't be fighting the custody case in court. I should be just letting my wife have her way and have what she wanted. On that ride, every issue that I brought up, he had one or two scripture references that he referred me to, which answered my worries and concerns.

We know that as we cope with life, as the enemy attacks us with negative feelings, or thoughts in various situations, all we need to do is to find the appropriate scripture verse that says the opposite and apply that scripture verse in warfare. Well, this businessman was doing it for me with every issue and everything that I brought up about my life that was a problem. He was bringing one or two scripture verses to encourage me and by the time I dropped him off, I was really uplifted. He signed a cheque. It's called a cab charge in Australia, but it's like a chequebook just for taxis. He signed one of them, got his briefcase, and then bid goodbye. He said it was a pleasure meeting me and that he'd pray for me.

I pulled my taxi off the curb and drove about fifty feet and then pulled over. I told myself, "That has to be an angel!" I ran back into the airport to where the check-in counters were and looked everywhere. He wasn't there. I ran to the toilets to check and he wasn't there. I ran upstairs to the departure lounge. I looked everywhere in that airport and I couldn't find him. He had just disappeared into thin air. Once again, I had met an angel and he'd seriously inspired me. As I look back into that encounter, I still remember a warm glow and the feeling that he had given me. I've been used to counsel people and give directions and encouragement, and I've been really used to minister to a person before. This time, an angel came down and ministered to me.

One thing you'll find if you read a book on angels, or if you read accounts of angels, they'll often disappear. They'll just disappear and the person can't find them, or can't see them after they've had their encounter. Many people can't prove that what they saw was an actual angel during their experience. They just know it in their hearts. They just know that it was an angel.

Those are the first four encounters that I had with angels.

As I prepare this short eBook, I am touched by the stories that I have shared. I want to let you know that I am just a simple man. I am no big name preacher with a big following. I am just one of you. I am just a person who loves Jesus.

Reflections

Story 1

It took real faith, the faith of a child, to ask for my angel to hold my hand in the first story. But the faith of children constantly amaze us. It is a really special memory and something that I am glad about. You may notice that the idea of holding my angel's hand might not have come from this little boy, but may have originated from the Holy Spirit. I think that the Holy Spirit is active in many ways in our lives, without us openly acknowledging it.

Story 2

In the second and third encounters, with the help of the Holy Spirit and Jesus speaking to me, I learned the lesson not to judge people. It took me years from those encounters to become the person that I am today, when it comes to judgement; but it all started there. If someone wanted to say that my encounters are not what I thought they were, I would point them to the fruit in my life that came from it. It would be pretty good fruit from a deception, don't you think?

Story 3

It was the fourth encounter that showed me that God cares about me. I was touched so deeply that He would send an angel to counsel me. Years after this event, my ex-wife told me that I could no longer see my son. I told her I would see her in court. It was at this time that Jesus told me not to fight in court and to let my wife have her way. I didn't see my son for sixteen years after I had the courage to let my wife win. During those sixteen years, I was reminded often of this fourth encounter and how the businessman angel told me not to fight in court with my wife. The memory of that encounter kept me in peace, while I suffered from not seeing my son for so long. Last year, I saw my son and his wife, and I had a good time with them.

Angels can really bless you. Let's continue in the next chapter.

Chapter 2
Prophetic Angels

I hope you enjoyed chapter one.

Soon enough, at the right time in life, I received the ability to see through the Spirit, to be able to see angels in my room, in my house and at other places. I didn't have to meet them in the flesh. I could interact with them just through life.

Story 1 Gabriel Dictates Prophecy

One night, I was praying, talking to Jesus back and forth and a presence came into my room. I asked Jesus who the presence was and He said, "It's Gabriel."

I asked, "Is it Gabriel, the one who appeared to Mary and Daniel?"

Jesus said, "Yes, now get up. He has a scroll in his hand and he has a prophecy that I want you to release to the world. So get up, go to your computer and type the message."

I got up. I said hello to Gabriel. He said hello.

I was a bit shocked. I was really in awe that I was meeting such an important angel. I think for many messenger angels, their job and function is to deliver messages to Earth and to people. Gabriel is like the head of the messenger angels. He's the most important messenger in the Bible and the most important messages came through him.

I went to my lounge room. I sat down at my keyboard and opened up a Microsoft Word page. Gabriel just dictated the prophetic word that was on the scroll. It's simple as just listening to someone reading to you at the pace that you can type and he was just reading the message from God. At the time, I was posting on a website called Ezine Articles. That was a popular website where you can publish your articles, so you didn't have to maintain a blog. They will distribute and put it out there for people to read.

People who have their own blogs and websites can read your articles and copy and paste it and if they did it the proper way that Ezine Articles suggested, it would come up that the article had been shared one time on another blog. Well, this article, this prophecy, was shared 153 times. Up till that time, some of my articles that were very good had been shared about twenty times. This was a real spike in the numbers and it was proof to me that 153 websites thought that this was the angel Gabriel speaking and this was a true Prophetic Word. It's also interesting to note that 153 is the amount of fish that were caught by the disciples, when they counted the fish on the beach with Jesus.

It wasn't 152, it wasn't 154, it wasn't 167 – it was a Biblical number, 153.That was like another sign to me that it was an anointed word of God. So that was the time I met Gabriel.

People may look at this story and say to themselves that I could not have met such an important angel of Heaven. And believe me, it is easy to see their point. But we need to remember that God doesn't look at a person's status. It says in Scripture - at least three times that I know of - that God treats everyone equally. I would also have trouble understanding that this angel was Gabriel, even today. Though when 153 blogs re-posted that prophecy, I was sure that my encounter was real. The number never went higher than 153. It stayed there for years.

Now, how do you see an angel? If I just tell you to think of a pink elephant, straight away, you get a picture of an elephant in your mind. Well, the way you can see that pink elephant is the same way you can see an angel. If I say now that the pink elephant just sat down on a big trailer and he's going to get transported, you can see the trailer, and the truck that's going to tow it, and you can see the elephant in the trailer.

The way that you see those things in your mind, that's how you can see visions. You see things on the movie screen of your mind. If you want to learn how to see a spirit like that, to be able to interact and have and see visions, there's a book called *Seeing in the Spirit Made Simple* by a man called Praying Medic, who's a friend of mine. That book will teach you how to do it. That's one prophetic angel who came with a prophetic message.

Story 2 Prophetic Angels

I have about four different styles of doing Prophetic Words. One of the styles that God gets to use is to bring an angel with a scroll. The angel would just appear in my house with a scroll when I was going to do a Prophetic Word. I'd sit down at my computer, do dictation and the angel would essentially read a message from God for that person to me.

It was a very un-stressful way of doing a Prophetic Word because I didn't have to think. I didn't have to worry about whether I was getting the Prophetic Word right, or forming my sentences properly. All I had to do is take dictation and type what I heard that the Spirit dictated. The people who received those Prophetic Words were blessed and they had no idea that an angel had delivered their Prophetic Word. I supposed they would have been blessed if those people had known. That's another way that angels can be used as a messenger and I've seen plenty of those angels deliver the Prophetic Words like that.

Over the years, I have become very comfortable with meeting angels and I am sure that for a year or so, God had me prophesy using angels for me to get very comfortable with meeting them.

Story 3 Prophet's Angel

You met Michael, my guardian angel, in the first chapter. The first story I told was about my guardian angel.

Well, my guardian angel got promoted. During the course of my life, he became a prophetic angel with a prophetic anointing, who carries the anointing that I move in as a prophet. When I move in prophecy, Michael comes with me. Sometimes, Michael can fully manifest his power and his anointing in my life. When he does this, I can go into a state where I can walk through a shopping center and have a Prophetic Word for every person I see. I can know something about every person I see. The first time it happened was in Brisbane, Australia. I walked into a shopping center and I knew something about every person I see, enough to go and deliver a Prophetic Word to them.

I had enough knowledge about every stranger to go and deliver a prophecy to them, and I really had fun during that day. I had to fill in six hours, because I was staying at a person's place and they told me to come back in six hours. I led six people to the Lord that day. I led five young girls to the Lord and one guy who was a Baptist and Christian, and I led him back to Jesus. That was one of the most productive days I had in the ministry of prophetic events. That was because Michael had fully manifested in my life that day. I can ask Michael to manifest himself and bring on that 100% anointing, so I can deliver a Prophetic Word to anyone that I see in a shopping center.

Michael is specialized in that anointing. He's still my guardian angel, but he has an extra ability. It's like a man can be a woman's husband, plus the pastor of the church. One of him is his relationship and another one is his anointing and ministry calling. Michael has a guardian angel relationship with me, but he also has a ministry anointing for my life. There are the prophetic angels and I hope that you were blessed by this chapter.

Reflections

Story 1

It is not through pride that I share that I have met Gabriel and had him minister through me. Instead, it is done with great humility. I am only too aware that people who read this book are going to take exception with it. I know that some people may even write bad reviews. So what is the fruit? I believe what I got from it was that it made me very special to the Lord. I felt so honored to have such an important messenger come to me. I am humbled that the Lord used me to give such an important corporate Word to the West. In years past when I was full of pride, I may have boasted about this encounter; today, it humbles me to share it.

Story 2

Having prophetic angels come to me shows me that I have the ability any time that I am called to prophesy, even if I have to call upon an angel to get the Prophetic Word. Meeting so many of these angels with Prophetic Words bore the fruit in my life of me being very comfortable in the presence of angels. I also came to realize that every angel has a purpose and they loved to be used and to interact with humans.

Story 3

Having Michael in my life brings me great comfort. There was a time when I have waned the anointing to prophesy over many people, I have called him to manifest his anointing to me again. The fruit of having him in my life is that many people, hundreds of people, have been blessed by a Spirit-filled Word of life to encourage them. I am now confident in years to come when I minister in a church, that I will be able to call him and minister over a hundred people, or more as needed.

Chapter 3

Protection Angels

This chapter is going to be on the subject of protection. How have I interacted with angels when they've come in the form of protection for my life? We know that one of the ministries of angels is protection and these stories demonstrate that part. Let us start with the first story.

Story 1 Youth Back Down

One time, I was giving a homeless person a meal in McDonald's, we'd eaten our meal and I'd gone up to get him a coffee after his meal. As I came back, I saw something fly through the air towards the homeless man. It came from two youths that were there. I asked the homeless man, "Did they throw something at you?"

He said, "Don't worry about it."

I said, "No, I'm going to worry about it. What did they throw at you?"

And he said, "A napkin."

I rose to my feet and addressed the two youths, and I said, "Did you throw something at him?"

They stood up and said to me, "Do you want to go outside? Do you want to make something of it?"

Initially, I was afraid because I'm not a fighter and they were quite scary. Then, faith ascended, I got bold and I said with confidence, "We can go outside, but if two people that you can't see start hitting you and punching you, and the punches aren't coming from me, but from something you can't see, just know that you are warned that they were my angels, protecting me."

Both guys went white as a ghost with fear and started stuttering, "Please leave us alone. We're sorry."

I said, "Tell the homeless man you're sorry,"

They shouted out to the homeless man that they were sorry. They asked him to forgive them. They said they were sorry about what they did. Then, they sat down, and said, "We don't want any trouble. Please leave us alone."

I was really shocked by that and years later, in a conversation with the Lord, I asked about these occurrences, this one, and another one that I'm about to share.

The Lord Jesus said that even though I couldn't see the angels, when I said to those people that something they can't see will start to hit them, they saw two angels, six foot seven and about four feet across in the chest, with big forceps and muscles all over, flexing their muscles at them. The angels are normally dressed in leather vests showing all their biceps. They appear to these guys and were basically saying with their looks, "we're going to punch you out." That's what the guys saw and they went white as a ghost, and were full of fear.

If you follow angel stories, we often hear or read in books that people have backed off and been scared. But the people who are getting protected don't actually see the angels protecting them. They only realize it when they hear the accounts of the people who threatened them ask, "Who were those big men that were with you?"

They find out second hand that they had angels with them. All they did was pray.

I spoke out boldly and angels appeared to the two threatening youths.

People may say that if I had just let the napkin throwing incident alone and said nothing, I would have not needed the angels. But I don't think we, as Christians, are meant to let injustice happen when we can prevent it. At the time of this incident, I did not know that angels had appeared. It was only later when I asked the Lord about this incident and the next one I am going to share with you, that the Lord told me what had gone on. This shows me that we don't always need to know when angels are protecting us; it is just important that they do.

Story 2 Bouncer Freaks Out

Here is a similar story. I was with an indigenous New Zealand person; he'd been drinking too much so he was drunk. We came out to the front of a hotel/pub and as we were coming, the security guard/bouncer at the front of the hotel started to pick on him.

I said, "He's with me, so if you're picking on him, you're picking on me."

The security guard was getting ready to hit me, when I felt my confidence rising up and I said to him, in a loud voice, "Turn around."

He turned around.

I said forcefully, "See that light pole up there?"

And he nodded.

I said, "That's where you're going to land if you hit me. Something you can't see is going to hit you and that's where you're going to land."

His face turned white, full of fear. He said, "Please leave. I don't want to cause any trouble. I'm sorry. Please leave." He said this with a stuttering, frightened speech. Once again, like I'd encountered those two guys at McDonald's the first time, this was the second time I saw someone who wanted to be violent with me go to water and become scared.

And so once again, an angel manifested next to me. The security guard and the two youths didn't directly look at the angel. They look at you, but they become terrified. They can see the angel next to you, but they keep addressing you with their eyes. This was the second occasion that angels protected me and my friend.

Story 3 Spiritual Hunt

The third story that I want to share in this chapter may be hard for you to believe. One time, I was at this church and I had a couple of people who were with me. I had a band of disciples. I had about four people with me. We went to this healer's church that runs on a Saturday night.

At the end of the service, we went up to the front for prayer and the guy next to me - one of my friends - said he had a pain in his leg. The healer was busy praying for someone else and so I asked Jesus, "What do I do?"

Jesus said. "Just lay your hand on his leg and say, I rebuke you, Jezebel."

So I laid my hand on his leg and I said, "I rebuke you, Jezebel."

As soon as I did that, one of the women in the room levitated. She rose from the ground. She was on the ground from praying. She rose and went about ten inches off the ground, across the floor, for about five feet, screaming at the top of her lungs. That got the healer's attention and he knew that it came from me. But he did nothing about it. They had coffee afterwards, whereas my group left early. I was afraid the lady who had levitated with the Jezebel spirit was going to cause some troubles, since that's what normally happens when a Jezebel gets identified.

I just had a spiritual sense that something was wrong and was going to be trouble, so I led the guys away from the train station. I led them into another street and I felt spiritually that there was a spiritual hunt that was going on. In witchcraft circles, sometimes, they can call on everyone and attract the wrong spirit. These spirits can tell people what those who are being hunted look like, so people come from everywhere to hunt and harm the spirit's prey. I'd been in one of these hunts before and experienced it, so spiritually, I was aware that it was happening again to me and today, my friends did, too. I told them about it and what was happening.

One of the guys started to moan. He started to cry almost. I said, "Please be quiet. I'm sure that angels can come and stop us from being seen, but I'm not sure we can block out your sound."

But he kept on moaning. I thought of running away from him, leaving him behind, and letting him get beaten up. While I was trying to work that out, a woman came out of a second story apartment above us and took her top off. She was naked, showing her breasts and for four young men, that was a good sight and certainly something that would normally keep four guys transfixed. I knew then from the woman's behavior that the people hunting us knew our location.

I was sure it was just a matter of minutes before violent people arrive and I didn't know if angels can muffle the sound of my friend crying. I was very annoyed with him. At that point, I hadn't seen angels before, but I was aware they were there. I turned my attention to the guy with us who'd been at my house and seen angels. I asked the Lord to open his eyes to see the angels around us.

His spiritual eyes were opened and he said the whole street is full of angels. He said "In fact, that cloud up there isn't a cloud. It's an army an angels waiting to help." He said, "You're alright."

I asked him, "So we can walk out of here?"

He replied, "Yeah."

My friend was still moaning. He didn't believe that.

He didn't believe the testimony that we were safe. He was still moaning and I was pushed to the extreme. Jesus is in charge of a lot of things, but Michael is in charge of the army of the Lord. I was pushed to my limit and I said, "Michael, come here!"

The guy who can see the angels started screaming at the top of his lungs and he fell to his knees. We knew something was in front of him and he was screaming at its presence. If I was worried about my friends whimpering, this scream outdid that. The angels must have been able to stifle sounds, because this guy's screaming was amazing. It's a proper account of how people normally react when they meet angels. They're full of fear. My friend fell to his knees and screamed. I declared peace over him and he grew quiet.

I said, "Can you ask the angel in front of you if his name is Michael, the Archangel?"

My friend replied "Yes. You already know that."

I said, "Can you ask him if it's safe for us to walk out of here and the people that are coming for us can't see us?"

My friend said, "Yes, Michael says it's safe. The angels will protect you. You can walk to the station now and everything is going to be okay."

My other friend, who had been moaning, had stopped and was in his right mind, primarily because he had been convinced that Michael had come due to the screaming and the other guy quaking with fear. I was also comforted, as I knew now that the angels can not only walk with us and keep others from seeing us, but I knew now that they can also hide sounds.

You may not know, so I will tell you here. When a group of angels walk with you, it is possible to be hidden from view from those meaning to harm you. The hunt had not been called off, but the evil people looking for us simply could not see us anymore.

I got the guys together, said thank you to Michael and we started walking. I felt Jesus come and walk beside us. I was really thankful for the guy who saved the day. I was so happy about the guy who'd helped us, who had the spiritual sight. I asked him if he'd like to meet Jesus and he said yes. And I said, "Just stand here." He stood over the side of the road.

I asked Jesus, "Can you appear to him?"

Jesus said "Sure, I'd love to."

We saw our friend who was standing drop to his knees and he was just talking into thin air for about five minutes. He was talking and when he got up, he had tears in his eyes. He told us that it was the most awesome experience he'd ever had in his life and that he was so amazed.

The angels stayed with us all the way into the city. When we arrived at our destination, the woman, Jezebel, was there and she launched another hunt. This time, the Holy Spirit showed me how to deal with each person who came to cause us trouble.

Story 4 Saved From Murder

Another occasion that angels protected me was when I became homeless in the infamous Red Light District of Australia called King's Cross. I used to go there and minister to the prostitutes in this strip joint/brothel. When I did, I used to take some chocolates for them. The leadership of the King's Cross brothel used to let me in. A friend of mine said that they would have thought I was a federal policeman. He said, "That's why they never hurt you."

One day, I went in homeless and one of the girls in the brothel let me sleep in her room. So it became obvious to the owners of that brothel that I wasn't a federal policeman, because a federal policeman wouldn't do that. The next day, they arranged to have some men maul me when I went off to another brothel to have a few drinks. One of the bouncers who got angry at me came up to the club and said he wanted to talk to me. "Do you want to go for a walk?" he said. To reassure me he said "I'm not going to hurt you."

I said, "Fine."

We went for a walk and had gone behind the original club. Before I know it, three guys were waiting for us and the bouncer said, "I'm just going to make a call on my phone and find out what you said to the owner about me."

As soon as he said that, the three guys started to hit me and I was soon on the ground. You've probably seen on TV or on video, three guys kicking another. They started to kick me and I was on the ground, saying sorry to the bouncer.

46

They were kicking me and I was apologizing. Then, I heard Jesus asked me, "Are you finished apologizing?"

I said, "Yeah."

Jesus continued, "They have a baseball bat there next to the dumpster. And when you're unconscious from the kicking, they're going to kill you. Are you ready to get up and run?"

I said, "Yeah."

I got up and ran from there to the police station. The police took me into the brothel and got my bag, then took me into the city, away from that.

After that account, I asked Jesus what happened and He said that when I got up, angels held the arms of the guys who were hitting me, so they couldn't grab me while trying to get up. It's impossible for a guy to be on his feet when three guys are kicking him. It's not viable for one to get away, but I did and I only got a bruised rib out of that. They had steel cap boots and they were prepared for what they did. They're well used to killing people.

Jesus told me that two angels had laid on either side of me and stopped the beating and kicking. The two angels shielded me from the actual blows of the kicks.

That was real intervention by angels. Later on, the police asked me about the club and asked if they were dealing drugs and I said, "Of course, they are and you know full well." I was talking to the owner of the club about six weeks later and he said, "It's dangerous for you to be in King's Cross. We kill people here."

I replied, "Well, you tried to kill me once and I'll take my chances."

Jesus told me to continue visiting the suburb until He says not to and not to fear man, but to fear Him, so I continued. I even went into the club a couple of times when Jesus told me to and all the people in that place were stunned that I've returned because they had tried to kill me. It was just a testimony to Jesus.

I had talked to the actual bouncer through the next year and he denied that anything had happened between us.

On New Year's Eve, everyone was going around, hugging each other, shaking each other's hands and wishing each other well. The bouncer came up to me and we hugged each other and we said all is well. Jesus told me that night that I can leave King's Cross and not visit anymore. He just wanted to restore that relationship with the bouncer. I had been a good witness to the prostitutes and been a shining light for Jesus in the club. Jesus simply wanted me to restore my relationship with the bouncer. He didn't want the bouncer to know that I was scared of anything, and wanted him to know that I stood up for my Jesus.

Before that last incident, I used to go into to King's Cross five/six nights a week, stay up all night and drink Coca Cola, witness to the prostitutes and just be their friend.

Story 5 Angels Hide Me

One day, I was going to do an intervention in one of the prostitute's life. She had reached a state where I thought she was ready to come out of her lifestyle. I was going to bring her home and let her dry out from heroin use. I was walking up the road towards King's Cross and a known person with a Jezebel spirit was across the road. She was watching me walk up. I thought to myself, "She's going to spoil what I'm doing."

Jesus said to me, "She can't see you!"

I argued with Jesus and I said, "Her eyes are following me. She's watching me walk up the road. What do you mean she can't see me?"

Jesus said, "She's watching four anointed angels walk up the road and what she can see are four men walking up the road. She knows they're anointed and she's attracted to them, but she can't see you. You're in the middle of them and she can't see you."

That was another time where I saw an enemy of mine, someone who caused me trouble, watching me and I disappeared from her plain sight. When Jesus wants you to disappear, he can just bring angels around you and you can become invisible to a person, and the angels become the visible ones.

That was a way Jesus used to disappear in a crowd. A number of angels used to come around Him. He'd disappear and the angels would walk Him out of there.

Reflections

Story 1

It is comforting to know that God is ready to protect you in every situation that you find yourself in. Standing up for the homeless man's honor was the right thing to do. Injustice needs to be stood up against. When the two youths threatened me, I was genuinely scared. Not being a male who can fight, they were imposing figures to me. But my faith soared and being led by the Holy Spirit, boldness emerged in me and I declared that they would be in danger if they took me outside to fight. I found it interesting that the youths did not say that they saw the angels appear next to me as I warned them; their faces went pale and they started to stammer that they didn't want trouble from me. The lesson in this is that we don't need to see that we have protection, we just need to be sure that God promises it to us.

Story 2

When the security/bouncer was about to hurt my friend, the Christ in me naturally stood up for my friend who was drunk and couldn't defend himself. My friend did nothing to deserve the unwarranted attention from the bouncer. The bouncer was over six feet tall, had a big build and was used to violence. When I spoke by faith, I did it with confidence that my threat was going to sort the bouncer out. I had no idea that the bouncer was actually going to see an angel tower over him. I find it very fascinating that the bouncer didn't take his eyes off me, as he stammered for me and my friend to leave him. He didn't acknowledge with his eyes that he can see an angel. With this encounter, I was made confident that angels could indeed protect me. I don't go looking for fights, I am a naturally loving person, who is in no way prone to being violent. But I am happy when I have come up against it, Jesus has seen that I was protected.

Story 3

In the next story, I spoke about a spiritual hunt. It is my prayer that you never have this happen to you. On one occasion before this story, the same occurrence happened to me and Jesus and angels had protected me, so I was prepared for this one spiritually. In the first experience, angels had guarded me from a man in a car who had come with intent of violence and would have possibly killed me. The man had driven past me in a car three times, before he gave up and sped away. He never stopped his car and got out to attack me because I had some big men/angels with me that he knew he couldn't overpower. When I felt through the Spirit that this was a second hunt, I knew that we were going to have supernatural protection. What I didn't count on was one of my friends whimpering with fear. While I am led by the Spirit most of the time, I don't always have answers. Calling on Michael, the Archangel, was done through pure frustration and fear. I don't adhere to the fact that anyone can call on him and expect him to come. Never before have I seen a person scream with fear in the presence of an angel. I was shown that day that Michael carries immense power and authority. If I didn't have the whimpering friend, or if I had known that angels surrounding you could also mute sounds, as well as hide you, I would never have called on Michael. But I am happy that Jesus knows exactly what we need and when we need it, and He was quite able to accommodate me. I am happy and confident to face any spiritual hunt in the future.

Story 4

Of all my protection stories, I am so glad that Jesus had two angels lay on either side of me, when I was getting kicked to death. I only came out of that incident with one bruised rib. If two angels had not been by my two sides protecting me, all of my ribs would have been broken. I will be forever grateful that Jesus saved my life that day. The fact that I was able to get off the ground and get away from the three attackers meant that angels held the arms of the three attackers as I got up and got away. Knowing that God saved my life that day shows me that I have a great future ahead of me that He wants me to live for. Some people may be amazed at this story, but give your praise to Jesus, as this is what He does to keep His servants alive.

Story 5

The last one is simply a story of Jesus making me appear invisible. You will remember that a few times, people wanted to kill Jesus and Jesus disappeared though the crowd. This is how He did it. Angels dressed as men appeared around Him and He walked among them until He was safely away.

Jesus can and will use angels to protect those people who are His. It is my prayer that this chapter showed you the truth of that!

Chapter 4

Visiting Angels

I hope that you've been enjoying my stories in this book. I want you to know that meeting angels doesn't have to be something strange, or something unique. You can certainly have a life where you can meet and interact with them.

Story 1 Finance Angel

I remember reading a book about ministering with angels and I recall reading that we can have one that is like an angel for finances.

The book said that you can ask the angel his name, and then you can request that they go and get finances for you. I introduced myself to this angel called Mark, who's my finance angel. I told him to go and get me four hundred and fifty dollars, because I needed it for publishing a book. I've written twelve books that are on Amazon under my name. Within a week, five hundred dollars came in from unexpected sources.

I didn't tell anyone about my need and suddenly, people were giving me money. Money just came in and it was amazing. I have never asked him again to go and get me money. I'm not a person who asks for things. That was very interesting. His name was Mark, he visits me and he's often around.

Story 2 Meeting the Cup Bearer

I was talking to a friend one Valentine's Day - the friend in the story who was whimpering in chapter three and I couldn't silence when he was scared - and we were in this shopping center early in the morning.

The shopping center suddenly filled up with about a hundred angels and I was amazed. I told my friend that the place just filled up with angels and to be quiet for a moment because I wanted to know why they were there. When he looked around, he couldn't see them and he kept on talking so I sort of zoned him out, and began to ask Jesus why the angels were there. Jesus told me that He loved me and this was His Valentine's Day present to me. That was so special. That was my favorite Valentine's Day of all that I had in my life. It was just so amazing.

Jesus said to me, "See, on the left hand side, there on the rows of seats on the left?"

I said, "Yeah."

He said, "See the forth seat back on the left hand side on the row?"

I said, "Yeah."

Jesus continued, "See the seat closest to the aisle. Can you see the angel sitting there?"

I said, "Yeah."

Jesus told me, "He's my cup bearer."

When I heard the word cup bearer, I just thought that was like a personal servant, like a personal steward angel to Jesus. I talked to my mom later on and she said a cup bearer in the king's time used to be the personal valet and serving angel, but he'd also taste the king's food and drink the king's wine, so no one could kill the king. The cup bearer would lose his life due to the poison, but the king would never die.

Jesus doesn't need protection from being poisoned, but a cup bearer is like a really close angel. He would be the closest angel to Jesus and would be his servant. As I looked at the cup bearer angel seated there, I worked out that it would be a job that I would like to do. I would like to be the personal servant for Jesus when He's on Earth.

I'd like to travel around with Him, lay His clothes out, get Him cups of tea, prepare His meals, and do all sorts of things for Him. I'd like to sit in every meeting with Him, listen to Him preach and be with Him for anything that He needs, to get Him a recorder if He needs one to record His voice with, or just to be His personal valet and help Him out. I realized that I'd never worked out a job that I'd like to do in eternity, but straight away, I recognized a job that I wanted to have and do.

As we're walking out of the building that day, I went up to the cup bearer and put my arm around him and I said, "I love you."

He told me that he loves me too and he loves the way I treat Jesus. I realize now that it still gets me emotional. I understand now that he's always been with Jesus whenever

Jesus visited me. He's been there, but he hadn't manifested. It gets me emotional. It's my favorite visitation by an angel. It's really special to my heart, simply because that role, that position, is something I'd wish to do. Wouldn't you like to be in that position with Jesus, to always be with Him, to be present when He's reflecting on what He's just said, to be there to discuss things in the private situation when He's away from everyone else? Just to be with Him in everything?

Story 3 Tears from Jesus

A year or so later, I was sitting in a McDonalds with another friend. My friend noticed a presence go behind our seat and asked, "Is that Jesus?"

I said no, that's Michael, the Archangel. Michael and Jesus have a similar anointing, similar authority on their lives."

Michael sat down and then another entity passed behind us and my friend asked, "Is that Jesus?"

I said, "Yeah, that's Jesus."

Jesus sat down. Another friend of ours was there and he heard my friend asking, "Is that Jesus?"

He doubted. He said what he'd do is he'd rebuke Jesus in Jesus' name and if Jesus didn't leave, then he'd accept it was Jesus. He said unless I rebuke Him in Jesus' name, he wouldn't believe.

I saw Jesus sitting there and I saw a tear. It was one of the most focused visions I've seen of Jesus. I saw a tear roll down Jesus' cheek. I asked Jesus in my mind, "What are you crying for, Jesus?"

Jesus said, "You can only take some people so far." I could tell now that Jesus was crying over my friend's disbelief.

Just then, another angel manifested. It was the cup bearer. Apparently, Jesus has two of them. He has twins who are cup bearers and on that day, I met the second one.

I've met both of them now and I'm very happy about it. If you're spiritual at all and you can talk to Jesus, and He talks back to you, you can ask Him if He has two cup bearers, and did Matthew meet them both?

I've never read in an angel book, by anyone prophetic, or anyone in ministry that talks about supernatural things, when they have talked about the cup bearers. That's why meeting them was a special thing for me and it really blessed me.

Story 4 My Revival Angel

I walked out of my front door one day and bumped into an eight foot angel. I said to him, "What are you doing out here?"

He said, "I'm with you in your house."

I said, "I'm going to the shop."

He replied, "I'm coming with you."

I asked him, "What are you in my life for?"

He said, "I'm going to steward revival in your life and I'm going to be with you when you move and minister doing revivals."

I exclaimed, "That's amazing!"

His name is Elisha, like the one Elijah passed his ministry onto, Elisha. He lives in my house and He ministers through me on some of the things that I don't fully understand yet.

I still see him in my house nearly every day, when I pass my second bedroom. Every time that I leave my house to go to the shop for something, Elisha comes and chats with me.

Story 5 Michael's Modus Operandi

Another thing that I want to tell you is that Michael, the Archangel, can visit you on Earth and he can sit and talk to you. I've seen his generals. I've seen them come into a McDonald's store and get dispatched.

His generals are always getting orders dispatched to them, so Michael can be anywhere in the universe. He can always be operating, be it in Heaven or on Earth. He can be anywhere and dispatching orders to his generals. He can visit someone on Earth, talk to them, and interact with them, as well as run the angels under his authority at the same time.

One time, I met Michael and I asked him a question. I was meeting saints from Heaven and angels. I was asking each of them a question and when Michael came in front of us, I asked him, "Why is the world getting so dark?"

Michael said, "So people like you can shine brighter!"

I thought that was a really good answer for him to share with me. I hope that's really encouraged you and you've been blessed.

Reflections

Story 1

Most of the time, God supplies me with all the finances that I need for any given task. The time that I read about the financial angels, an angel called Mark manifested to me. I needed money and could have saved up the money, but seeing as Mark had shown himself to me, I thought I would test what this book said and ask him to get me the money I needed. Within a week, the full amount had come in from sources I was not expecting. I have not put Mark to work again, but miraculously, all my needs have been met since I met him the first time.

Story 2

I can still see the room full of angels in my mind's eye of that special Valentine's Day. It amazes me that Jesus can simply send a hundred angels to brighten your day. I will never forget meeting the cup bearer angel that day. I know that doing his job in eternity would be my dream come true. Jesus is aware that meeting that cup bearer remains as my favorite vision of all time and isn't disappointed with me for saying so. He alone knows what will satisfy our spirit-man.

Story 3

It was great to meet the second cup bearer in this story. What I remember most about this encounter was my friend's doubt. I remember Jesus' tears as they rolled down His cheek. Sure, rebuking a vision of Jesus might be a way to make sure you are not fooled by an impostor, but when I saw Jesus cry that day, I was sure I would never do it.

Story 4

Having Elisha in my house is cool. Every time I go past my spare bedroom, I sense him in there. Every time I go down to the shop to get supplies, he goes with me. He is a powerful angel and I know that he does a lot in my ministry at the moment; I am just not sure what he does though. We as humans want the answers to everything and many readers may want to know what he is doing in my life. I don't need to know. I am just happy to have him around. I know it has been prophesied that one day, I will cause revivals in ministry and I know in those days, Elisha will be supporting me all the way.

Story 5

I asked Jesus once why I had met Michael so many times and had met important saints from the Bible. He told me that I was having all these encounters to build my faith. It makes a lot of sense to find out that when Michael is visiting someone on Earth, he is also carrying out his duty and dispatching work as he meets with you. People may scoff at my stories and think that there is no way that I have met with one of Heaven's most powerful angels. All I can say in my defense is that God clearly says in Scripture no less than three times that He does not discriminate.

Final Thoughts

Some of you may be shaking your heads by now, wondering what you should do with this book. It is my prayer that the Holy Spirit may comfort you.

To those who were encouraged, I suggest books by Praying Medic and Michael Van Vlymen on "How to see in the spirit" so you, too, can interact with the supernatural. Both authors agree that the common person can meet and interact with angels.

I have been saved for forty years in 2015, and I am forty eight years of age as of writing, which means I was born again at the age of eight. I must confess that though this book is about angels, I have met Jesus on Earth and Heaven hundreds of times. There remains nothing that I wouldn't do for Jesus. I am a radical believer whose whole life is dedicated to Him. I feel that a book like this is important. I believe that too many books about angels are written by New Age people and I feel that it is high time that Christians start to write about angelic encounters.

I am going to endeavour to make this book 99 cents on Kindle and have it enrolled in Kindle Select, so I can make it free to download at least one day per month. Seeing that I have made it as cheap as I can at 99 cents, I ask that you tell your friends about it on Facebook, if you enjoyed it.

The subject of angels is always going to be controversial. Some people with testimonies of angelic encounters therefore keep those accounts to themselves, for fear of being mocked. It is my prayer that you get in touch with me and share your stories.

Whilst I had a couple of really scary stories in this book, I want you to know that God is more than able to protect us. Satan knows that I am going to do his kingdom great damage in the future and he simply tries his best to take me out. I have had to run to save my life three times and those times, a police station was within a short running distance.

I praise God for my life and I am so happy that He chooses to use me as He does. It is a great honor to serve God. I pray that this book has encouraged you to know that angels are real and a great deal to ordinary people like me.

Impartation Prayer

Dear Father

With the Biblical examples of Moses imparting his anointing to Joshua, and Elijah imparting his mantle to Elisha, I ask that you please impart my ability to see into the supernatural to the readers who have read this book and who desire this ability. Open the spiritual eyes of the dear readers who are hungry for more and let each of them be able to write to me and share their new encounters. I ask that you answer this prayer for me. I ask in Jesus' mighty name. Amen.

I'd Love to Hear from You

One really easy way to bless me is to write a short and honest review of this book on Amazon. It costs you nothing and it is a really wonderful way of letting other people know that this was an encouraging book to read. Before I buy any book personally, I make sure that I read the reviews on Amazon and if I am convinced by them, I make my purchase. I won't even download a free book, unless it has good reviews.

I personally read all the reviews that my books get and you can be sure that I will read your review.

Please feel free to also share a link to my book on Facebook with your friends, sharing in a short note with them why they would enjoy it.

To contact me:

You can write to my email address at
survivors.sanctuary@gmail.com.

You can donate money to my book writing ministry, or request a personal prophecy at
http://personal-prophecy-today.com.

Other Books by Matthew Robert Payne

If you enjoyed this book, you may enjoy other books by Matthew Robert Payne.

The Parables of Jesus Made Simple

The Prophetic Supernatural Experience

Prophetic Evangelism Made Simple

His Redeeming Love – A Memoir

Writing and Self Publishing Christian Nonfiction

Your Identity in Christ

Coping with your Pain and Suffering

Living for Eternity

Great Cloud of Witnesses Speak

Jesus Speaks Today

You can find these books at my Amazon author page at this link: http://tinyurl.com/pcqb66f

About the Author

Matthew was born again at the age of eight in a Baptist Church and quickly developed the ability to speak to Jesus, and have Jesus speak back to him. With a life that has seen much sorrow, he has developed a keen sense of compassion for all sorts of people.

Called as a prophet from birth, it wasn't till 2005 that he realized that he was called as a prophet. Over the past twenty years, he has been used by God to deliver over twenty thousand personal prophecies to people, the majority of which were given to total strangers. Matthew is well versed in hearing Jesus speak through him.

With an intimate relationship with Jesus, Matthew lives to lead people closer to the Jesus that he has come to know so well. Matthew does much of his teaching today on YouTube and through books on Amazon. Through this book, Matthew hopes people may come to trust Jesus and His angels better.

CPSIA information can be obtained
at www.ICGtesting.com
Printed in the USA
LVOW13s0236020517
532922LV00035B/1902/P